Swimming wi

Sand Tiger Sharks

CHRISTINE THOMAS ALDERMAN

BLACK
RABBIT
BOOKS

Bolt is published by Black Rabbit Books
P.O. Box 3263, Mankato, Minnesota, 56002.
www.blackrabbitbooks.com
Copyright © 2020 Black Rabbit Books

Marysa Storm, editor; Grant Gould, designer;
Omay Ayres, photo researcher

Library of Congress Cataloging-in-Publication Data
Names: Alderman, Christine Thomas, author.
Title: Sand tiger sharks / by Christine Thomas Alderman.
Description: Mankato, Minnesota : Black Rabbit Books, [2020] |
Series: Bolt. Swimming with sharks | Audience: Age 8-12. |
Audience: Grade 4 to 6. | Includes bibliographical references and index.
Identifiers: LCCN 2018037236 (print) | LCCN 2018037372 (ebook) |
ISBN 9781680728712 (e-book) | ISBN 9781680728651 (library binding) |
ISBN 9781644660508 (paperback)
Subjects: LCSH: Sand tiger shark–Juvenile literature.
Classification: LCC QL638.95.O3 (ebook) | LCC QL638.95.O3 A43 2020
(print) | DDC 597.3–dc23
LC record available at https://lccn.loc.gov/2018037236

Printed in the United States. 1/19

Image Credits

Alamy: Reimar, 12–13 (top), 24 (adult
sand tiger); Stocktrek Images, Inc., Cover; Steve
Woods Photography, 8–9, 16 (sand tiger), 23 (adult),
24 (sand tiger); commons.wikimedia.org: MusikAnimal,
32; fcda.us: FCDA, 14; iStock: Mark Kostich, 18–19 (tooth);
poco.cn: POCO Photography, 20; seapics.com: C & M Fallows,
28–29; Dough Perrine, 28; James D. Watt, 4–5; Jeff Rotman, 27;
Masa Ushioda, 17 (goblin); Toshio Minami, 18–19 (tooth); Shutter-
stock: 3DMI, 24 (larger shark); Brilliance stock, 24 (fish); Catmando,
17 (tiger shark); Dirk van der Heide, 16–17 (shark bkgd), 31; Eric
Isselee, 24 (smaller shark); Greg Amptman, 3; Jiang Zhongyan, 24
(fish); Joshua Haviv, 1; Kletr, 17 (hammerhead); Michael Rosskothen,
16 (great white); Pommeyrol Vincent, 6; saulty72, 11; Stefan Pircher,
12–13 (btm); Yongcharoen_kittiyaporn, 16–17 (water bkgd); iStock:
THEGIFT777, 6–7; sketchfab.com: rstr_tv, 16 (bull); tumblr.com:
Peter Chin, 22–23; uda.oceana.org: Oceana, 23 (baby), 24
(baby)
Every effort has been made to contact copyright holders
for material reproduced in this book. Any omis-
sions will be rectified in subsequent printings
if notice is given to the publisher.

Contents

CHAPTER 1

Swimming Along

Night falls in the ocean. Sand tiger sharks begin to stir. A large group comes together to hunt. They surround a school of fish. Circling the fish, the sharks **herd** them into a tall column of dinner. The fierce **predators** then dive in for the kill.

WEIGHT

UP TO 350 POUNDS
(159 kilograms)

What's in a Name?

The sand tiger shark's name comes from their skin and where they swim. These sharks have brown spots. They also spend their time swimming near the sandy ocean floor.

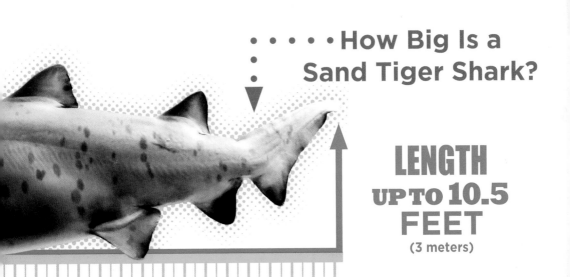

•••••• **How Big Is a Sand Tiger Shark?**

LENGTH UP TO 10.5 FEET
(3 meters)

DORSAL FINS

SPOTS

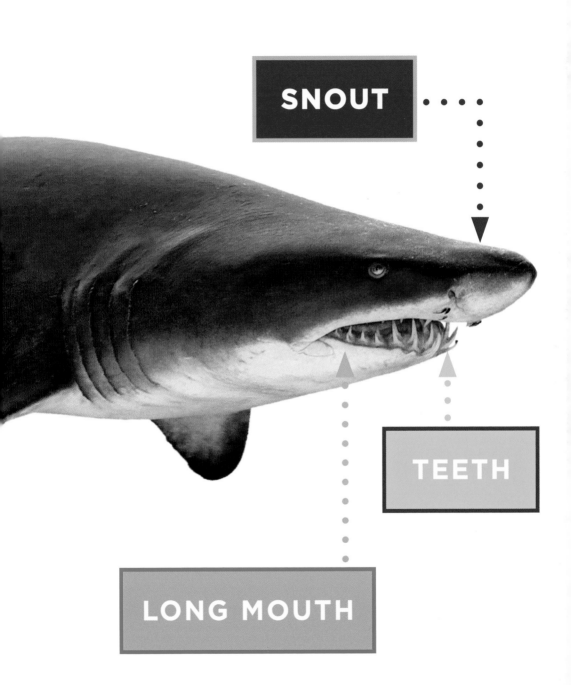

SNOUT

TEETH

LONG MOUTH

CHAPTER 2

Where They Live and What They Eat

Sand tigers live in many oceans. They swim mostly in warm **coastal** water. When seasons change and water cools, sand tigers swim to warmer water. These sharks have been tracked traveling hundreds of miles.

Sand tigers don't need to surface to breathe. But they do swallow air at the surface. They store the air in their stomachs. This air keeps them from sinking. They use it to float motionless in the ocean.

Sand Tiger Shark Range Map

Shipwreck Surprise

Sand tigers swim around the ocean floor. These sharks are silent and slow, but animals should still watch out. The sharks have incredible senses of touch, hearing, and smell. They slip through shipwrecks and hide in caves. They wait until **prey** comes near. Then the sharks strike.

Like other sharks, sand tigers can sense electricity created by prey.

SHARKS BY DEPTH

Different types of sharks swim at different depths in the water.

feet below surface	BULL SHARK	SAND TIGER SHARK	GREAT WHITE SHARK
0			
500			
1,000	Surface to 492 feet (150 m)		
1,500		shallow water to 625 feet (191 m)	
2,000			
2,500			surface to more than 820 feet (250 m)
3,000			
3,500			
4,000			
4,500			

HAMMERHEAD SHARK

TIGER SHARK

GOBLIN SHARK

surface to about 902 feet [275 m]

shallow water to 1,148 feet [350 m]

131 to 4,265 feet [40 to 1,300 m]

Many Meals

Sand tiger sharks often eat fish they can swallow whole. But these sharks aren't picky eaters. They also dine on crabs and stingrays. They snag slippery prey, such as squid, with their pointed teeth. Sand tiger sharks even eat other sharks.

People also call these sharks
spotted raggedtooth sharks. This name
comes from the sharks' teeth.

Scientists believe some sand tiger sharks might meet at shipwrecks to **mate.**

CHAPTER 3

Family Life

Scientists don't know much about sand tiger sharks' family lives. Some sand tigers live alone. Others live in small or large schools. They sometimes hunt together.

Baby Food

Sand tiger sharks have families slowly. Females only have babies every two years. And they only have one or two pups at a time.

There's a reason they have few pups. Pups eat their **siblings**! Many eggs develop inside mother sharks. Before they're even born, the largest babies eat the others. The extra food helps the pups grow big. Being larger at birth means they'll have fewer predators.

COMPARING SIZES

ADULT SAND TIGER
up to 10.5 feet (3 m) long

BABY SAND TIGER
about 3 feet (1 m) long

Sand Tiger Shark Food Chain

This food chain shows what eats sand tiger sharks. It also shows what sand tiger sharks eat.

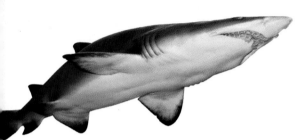

ADULT SAND TIGERS   **LARGER SHARKS**

SAND TIGER PUPS

ADULT SAND TIGERS

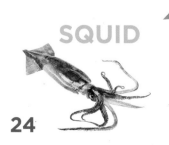

SQUID

FISH

SMALLER SHARKS

CHAPTER 4

Keeping Sharks Safe

Sharks are at the top of the food chain. Adult sand tigers don't have to worry about other animals. But they do have to worry about people. People are sharks' biggest **threat**. Humans fish too many sharks. More sand tigers die than are born. The population can't keep up!

Saving the Sand Tiger

People are taking steps to save sand tiger sharks. Some countries have rules to protect them. People must release any sharks they catch. Some countries have **banned** all shark fishing.

Sand tiger sharks often swim in aquariums. Being big and fierce makes them fun to watch. But it's not their real home. People must protect these sharks in the oceans.

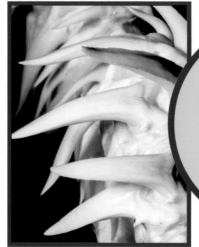

By the Numbers

8 TO 9 MONTHS

HOW LONG FEMALE SAND
TIGER SHARKS ARE PREGNANT

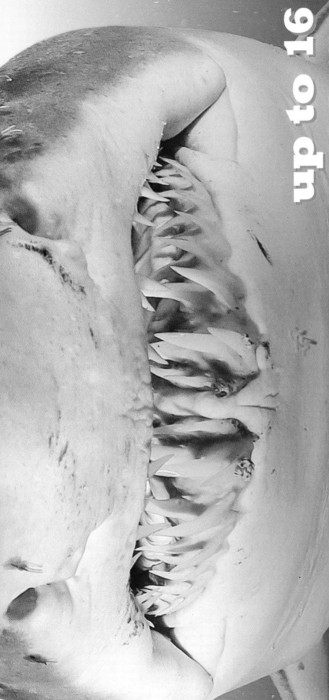

up to 16 years

LIFE SPAN
IN CAPTIVITY

about 100 million

NUMBER OF SHARKS KILLED BY
HUMANS EACH YEAR (ALL KINDS)

ban (BAYN)—to forbid by law

captivity (kap-TIV-i-tee)—the state of being kept in a place, such as a zoo

coastal (KOHS-tl)—near the shore

herd (HURD)—to gather and move animals or people into a group

mate (MAYT)—to join together to produce young

predator (PRED-uh-tuhr)—an animal that eats other animals

pregnant (PREG-nuhnt)—carrying one or more unborn offspring in the body

prey (PRAY)—an animal hunted or killed for food

sibling (SI-bling)—a brother or sister

snout (SNOUT)—the projecting part of an animal's face that includes the nose or nose and mouth

threat (THRET)—something that can do harm

BOOKS

Best, Arthur. *Sharks.* Migrating Animals. New York: Cavendish Square, 2019.

Centore, Michael. *Saving Ocean Animals: Sharks, Turtles, Coral, and Fish.* Protecting the Earth's Animals. Broomall, PA: Mason Crest, 2018.

Hutchison, Patricia. *Sharks Are Awesome.* Animals Are Awesome. Mankato, MN: 12 Story Library, 2018.

WEBSITES

Sand Tiger Shark
kids.nationalgeographic.com/animals/sand-tiger-shark/#sand-tiger-shark-close-teeth.jpg

Sand Tiger Shark
www.floridamuseum.ufl.edu/fish/discover/species-profiles/carcharias-taurus/

Sand Tiger Sharks | SHARK ACADEMY
www.youtube.com/watch?v=gHMSzIECvzE

INDEX